This document, referred to hereafter as "eBook", was written and published by Brenden Diaz in August 2020.[1]
© Copyright 2020.
All rights reserved.

---

[1] Opinions expressed are solely my own and do not express the views of others including, but not limited to, the State University of New York, University at Buffalo, the University of Oxford, Carl Frey, Michael Osborne, Benjamin Graham, David Dodd, Jason Zweig, Howard Schilit, amazon.com, and readyratios.com. The author claims no affiliation with the aforementioned entities. The author claims no rights to any of their material work, intellectual property, concepts, writing, trademarks, or copyrights. **This document is for educational purposes only.**

This page intentionally left blank.

Thank you to my hard-working wife, dedicated parents, and loving brothers who have always loved and supported me. It's because of you that I have learned the power of family and love. I am forever indebted to you.
-Brent

Ecclesiastes 4:9-12

Two are better than one,
because they have a good return for their labor:

If either of them falls down,
one can help the other up.
But pity anyone who falls
and has no one to help them up.

Also, if two lie down together, they will keep warm.
But how can one keep warm alone?

Though one may be overpowered,
two can defend themselves.
A cord of three strands is not quickly broken.

TABLE OF CONTENTS

INTRODUCTION	V
FUNDAMENTAL ANALYSIS	1
1. FIRST, DON'T LOSE	1
2. OBTAIN THE PRICE PER SHARE	3
3. OBTAIN EARNINGS PER SHARE	3
4. OBTAIN PRICE-TO-EARNINGS RATIO	3
5. CALCULATE COMPANY'S INTRINSIC VALUE	5
ASSETS	7
EARNINGS	9
DEFINITE PROSPECTS	12
FINAL NOTE ON INTRINSIC VALUE	16
6. RESEARCH INDUSTRY COMPETITORS	16
START YOUR INDUSTRY RESEARCH	18
7. CHECK FOR ACCOUNTING FRAUD	18
THREE TYPES OF ACCOUNTING MANIPULATION	19
DRAMATIC TRENDS	20
ACQUISITION CRAZY	21
AGGRESSIVE CHIEF	21
SKEPTICISM IS YOUR COMPETITIVE ADVANTAGE	21
QUICK REFERENCE GUIDE	i
ABOUT THE AUTHOR	ii
DEFINITIONS	iii
THANK YOU	vi

Read time: 45 minutes

INTRODUCTION

People achieve wealth through business or investing. This eBook will give you insight on how to analyze *business performance* so that your *investment performance* is optimized. When your *investment performance* is optimized, so is your *wealth production*.

This eBook appeals both to aspiring business owners and enterprising investors. How?

 If you are an aspiring business owner, by reading this eBook, you will understand the mind of an enterprising investor and you will learn the business aspects the investor will be keen on viewing in his fundamental analysis of your business. Even more, you will learn how the best managed companies are run by becoming privy to what makes companies attractive and investable.

 If you are an aspiring investor, by reading this eBook, you will gain proven investing insight from this survey of value investing–sourced from the foundational texts of the most successful investing practice in existence: *The Intelligent Investor* and *Security Analysis*, by Benjamin Graham and David Dodd.[2]

This eBook is to be read like a practical reference guide.

---

[2] Disclaimer: I do not own, nor claim to own, any of the intellectual property, concepts, or text in any edition and/or publication of *The Intelligent Investor,* and *Security Analysis,* by Benjamin Graham and David Dodd. This eBook, and the literary and/or graphical contents contained within, do not constitute, is not, and does not offer, financial advice, legal, and/or investing advice. This eBook, in its entirety, serves only as an educational review of the aforementioned texts, and their principles, with author commentary literarily incorporated. **This eBook is for educational purposes only.**

I do not spend time proving the value of fundamental analysis or value investing. If you are not *yet* convinced that value investing is the best investing strategy available, stop reading now, and purchase **The Intelligent Investor** and **Security Analysis**.[3] Once you have completely read both texts and have formulated an opinion, return to this eBook.

---

[3] Disclaimer: This is not a sponsored advertisement. I do not monetarily gain from any sales generated through this referral. I claim no affiliation with Benjamin Graham, David Dodd, their publishing agents, and/or amazon.com.

FUNDAMENTAL ANALYSIS

1. FIRST, **DON'T LOSE**

The priority of any investment operation is to maintain the safety of principal with an ample margin of safety. Avoiding serious loss is a precondition for sustaining a high compound rate of growth. From page 18 of *The Intelligent Investor*, "[a]n investment operation is one which, upon thorough analysis promises safety of principal and an adequate return. Operations not meeting these requirements are speculative." The primary way of achieving an ample margin of safety in investment operation is to purchase the investment security (common stock, preferred stock, bond) at a discount, relative to the stock's value. While the exact manner of discount calculation is never explicitly defined in the books published by Benjamin Graham (*Security Analysis* and *The Intelligent Investor*), suggestions do exist within these foundational texts. The following actionable steps embody the zeitgeist of those suggestions.

Page 523 of *The Intelligent Investor* provides some useful definitions before we proceed:

> Investment is most intelligent when it is most *businesslike*.
>
> [I]f a person sets out to make business profits from security purchases and sales, he is embarking on a business venture of his own, which must be run in accordance with accepted business principles if it is to have a chance of success.

The first and most obvious of these principles is "Know what you are doing–know your business." For the investor this means: Do not try to make "business profits" out of securities– that is, returns in excess of normal interest and dividend income–unless you know as much about security values as you would need to know about the value of merchandise that you proposed to manufacture or deal in.

A second business principle: "Do not let anyone else run your business, unless (1) you can supervise his performance with adequate care and comprehension or (2) you have unusually strong reasons for placing implicit confidence in his integrity and ability."

A third business principle: "Do not enter upon an operation– that is, manufacturing or trading in an item–unless a reliable calculation shows that it has a fair chance to yield a reasonable profit. In particular, keep away from ventures in which you have little to gain, and much to lose." For the enterprising investor this means that his operations for profit should be based not on optimism but on arithmetic. For every investor it means that when he limits his return to a small figure–as formerly, at least, in a conventional bond or preferred stock– he must demand convincing evidence that he is not risking a substantial part of his principle.

A fourth business rule is more positive: "Have the courage of your knowledge and experience. If you have formed a conclusion from the facts and if you know your judgement is sound, act on it–even though others may hesitate or differ." (You are neither right or wrong because the crowd disagrees with you. You are right because your data and reasoning are right.)

> To achieve *satisfactory* investment results is easier than most people realize; to achieve superior results is harder than it looks.

An excerpt from Graham's *Security Analysis* leads us well into the actionable steps of value investing:

> Of more practical importance is the question whether or not investment can be successfully carried on in common stocks that appear cheap from the quantitative angle and that—upon study—seem to have *average prospects* for the future. Securities of this type can be found in reasonable abundance, as a result of the stock market's obsession with companies considered to have unusually good prospects of growth. Because of this emphasis on the growth factor, quite a number of enterprises that are long established, well financed, important in their industries and presumably destined to stay in business and make profits indefinitely in the future, but that have no speculative or growth appeal, tend to be discriminated against by the stock market—especially in years of subnormal profits—and to sell for considerably less than the business would be worth to a private owner.

2. OBTAIN THE **PRICE PER SHARE**
(PPS = Market Capitalization/Outstanding Shares)

3. OBTAIN **EARNINGS PER SHARE**
(EPS = Annual Net Profit/Outstanding Shares)

4. OBTAIN **PRICE-TO-EARNINGS RATIO**
(PE = PPS/EPS)

According to Graham, a PE ratio higher than 20 is absolutely overpriced and not worth further investigation.

Consider the following thought experiment.

Let's assume you have a friend, friend A, who tells you he is willing to give you $1 every year, *ad infinitum*, provided you give him $20 right now.

Friend B overhears the exchange and rushes over with a similar offer, however Friend B says you don't have to give him $20. You only have to give him $3. Assuming you accept Friend B's offer, you will be given $1 every year, for the rest of your life.

Which deal sounds most attractive? Of course, Friend B's deal sounds much more attractive because, quite frankly, it's cheaper! You will have to wait a lot longer to get your initial investment, your *principal*, out of Friend A's deal as compared to Friend B's deal. Assuming no change in the annual $1 earnings–specifically–it will take you 17 years longer to regain your principal if you choose Friend A's deal.

Who in the world would want to wait that long to regain their money? No one!

Graham generously provides that if a reasonable PE ratio *upper limit* is 20, then a PE ratio of 12 serves as the suitable ratio of an average company with neutral prospects. Naturally, the closer the PE ratio gets to zero, *prima facie*, the more attractive the security becomes.

This understanding of security PE ratios should be adhered to through the entire investment operation: from inquiry, through purchase, ownership, and sale.

TIP: Remember, as an investment analyst, and prospective purchaser of corporate securities, you must not aim to profit from future change, rather, you must guard against it. The business future is a hazard, which your conclusions will encounter. The analyst should not poise their analytical conclusions in expectation of vindication–as taking this approach constitutes speculation (it violates the *adequate return* portion of the strict definition of investing due to unfounded expectations of substantial returns) and is an overall setup for disaster.

This is why Graham-Dodd value investors prefer cheaper stocks– stocks with lower price-to-earnings ratios–as these securities provide ample margins-of-safety, guarding them from a future where business earnings diminish, and the length of time required for principal recovery increase. Judging the investment merit of a security on the basis of its PE ratio serves less as an accurate judge of investment merit and more as a quantitative limiter, narrowing the pool of candidate securities available for investigation.

5. CALCULATE COMPANY'S **INTRINSIC VALUE**

Much easier said than done.

Graham is notoriously elusive in explicitly defining *intrinsic value*. This is due to the complex nature of defining a firm's intrinsic value, and its coinciding investment merit. Wisely, Graham provides a helpful analogy for the enterprising investor regarding the practice of defining a company's intrinsic value on page 497 of *Security Analysis* (6th edition):

> **Exact Appraisal Impossible.** Security analysis cannot presume to lay down general rules as to the "proper value" of any given common stock. Practically speaking, there is no such thing. The bases of value are too shifting to admit of any formulation that could claim to be even reasonably accurate. The whole idea of basing the value upon current earnings seems inherently absurd, since we know that the current earnings are constantly changing. And whether the multiplier should be ten or fifteen or thirty would seem at bottom a matter of purely arbitrary choice. But the stock market itself has no time for such scientific scruples. It must make its values first and find its reasons afterwards. Its position is much like that of a jury in a breach-of-promise suit; there is no sound way of measuring the values involved, and yet they must be measured somehow and a verdict rendered. Hence the prices of common stocks are not carefully thought out computations but the resultants of a welter of human reactions. The stock market is a voting machine rather than a weighing machine. It responds to factual data not directly but only as they affect the decisions of buyers and sellers.

With those decisions usually galvanized by emotion.

While I agree that precisely defining a company's value, according to some arbitrarily crafted formula, is absurd, the enterprising analyst need only define it's value insofar as it quips the analyst with the power of action, the ability to exact an informed, binary decision: whether to purchase the security, or not. On page 48 of *Security Analysis*, 6th Edition:

> The rub, then and now, is how to calculate that [intrinsic value] worth. I suspect the authors deliberately refrained from defining

intrinsic value, lest they convey the misleading impression that the value of a security can be precisely determined. Given the practical limits of people's ability to forecast (an earnings report, a romance, the weather, or anything), the authors urge that investors think in terms of a range of values. Happily, this is quite satisfactory for the purposes of investors. To quote Graham and Dodd: "It is quite possible to decide by inspection that a woman is old enough to vote without knowing her age or that a man is heavier than he should be without knowing his weight." (p. 66)

Graham does guide his readers to several items of interest, exhibits of factual information regarding the financial status of a firm under scrutiny, which can be found in financial statements and used to approximate a firm's intrinsic value.

TIP: Remember, we attempt to define *intrinsic value* because, as value investors guarding against the future via adequate margins-of-safety, we ideally want to pay less than intrinsic value!

As noted by Graham, the general items/exhibits include: assets, earnings, and definite prospects. Next, I will elaborate on each item's worth, with respect to the item's ability to flesh-out intrinsic value. (And, yes, a majority of these items are accounting items, naturally, as the native language of business is accounting. I recommend an Accounting 101 textbook if you are unfamiliar with the nature of these terms.)

ASSETS

First a look at asset accounts in the determination of investment merit. From the Graham-Dodd literature (both *Security Analysis* and

The Intelligent Investor), identifying book value serves as an analyst's anchor in fleshing-out intrinsic company value.

Simply, **Book Value** is defined as total assets minus total liabilities (Book Value = A - L). Alternatively, book value may be viewed as stockholder's equity, according to the fundamental accounting equation. You now have your first factual, numeric comparator by which to judge the reasonableness of a stock's price! You can use book value to craft a helpful ratio that identifies, specifically, what you are buying.

The ratio is Book Value divided by Outstanding Shares (Book Value/Outstanding Shares). Compare the calculated number (the quotient derived) to the security's price (PPS). Ideally, the price-per-share you pay should be less than quotient derived from dividing book value by outstanding shares. This would be a bargain stock!

The next asset account of interest deals with **Net Current Assets** (NCA; derived by subtracting Current Liabilities from Current Assets; this number ideally should be positive as this would imply the company has sufficient liquid reserves to pay current liabilities if they all were to be called at once). Once identified, NCA should be proportionally compared to outstanding shares in ratio form: NCA/Outstanding Shares. This ratio can be compared to the price-per-share.

Once again, the ideal scenario is one where the price you pay should be less than the value of the aforementioned ratio. Graham craftily uses analogy, on page 49 of *Security Analysis*, to demonstrate the attractiveness this ideal scenario: "This [buying a security cheaper than it's NCA] was akin to buying a home for less than the amount of money in the bedroom safe and getting to keep the safe as well!"

One of the last asset tests of a company's value, but certainly not the least, involves its cash asset account. This is one of the more intuitive tests of a company's value since the tangible worth of cash is very easy to understand. The ratio of cash, divided by outstanding shares, serves as an excellent test of a company's intrinsic value.

Using an example from *Security Analysis*, let's assume a company's common stock is selling at a market rate of $20 per share. You calculate the company's cash-to-share value as $20.66. This is a *prima facie* good deal as the deal promises a strong margin-of-safety, protecting your investment principal from loss, because the shares are selling less than the company's tangible worth.

In today's technologically-guided economy, it is challenging, albeit not impossible, to find bargain stocks with steep margins-of-safety. This is due to the availability of information, automated investment operations, and long-lasting bull markets. Hence, the arrival of bear-markets make value investors rejoice, as a depressed market forces the bargain sale of securities.

EARNINGS

The value investor need not precisely calculate the future revenue of a business to come to an investment decision. In the consideration of a security purchase, whether the security be a common stock, preferred stock, or bond, the value investor should always seek to sufficiently protect her investment from loss. With respect to revenue, Graham recommends the sensible analyst use the last 10 years of revenue data to establish a future revenue estimation.

As we proceed in our analysis of a stock, let us note that we have moved from the static financial representations of a balance sheet to the dynamic financial exhibits of a company's income statement which sum transactions over an accounting period (typically of either a year or quarter year). As the figures from an income statement represent summed transactions over a period of time, it is important that we use simple statistical methods to adjust for the natural variations in business accounts that occur in any business cycle.

Therefore, I find it critical that the intelligent investor use the median of the last 10 years worth of top-line revenue (e.g. 'sales', etc.). This removes a large portion of outlier effects that would have been present if we used the arithmetic average. This number (the median of the prior 10 years worth of revenue) should be used to further flesh-out investment merit, post asset analysis. In both *The Intelligent Investor* and *Security Analysis*, Graham warns his readers of being seduced by growing revenue trends over just a couple of years, and of entertaining the tempting conclusion that perhaps this growth in revenue will sustain indefinitely–rarely is this the case.

In fact, he points to countless examples of firms which revert to *average* revenue performance (I use *average* very loosely here, as we know I mean median) after a 2 to 3 year revenue growth trend. On page 567 of *The Intelligent investor*, Jason Zweig (Graham's commenter) shows how even established companies like IBM can appear to increase in revenue "permanently" for several years, only to return to their statistical center. This financial behavior belongs to a phenomena referred to, formally, as a *trend*, where a numeric (in this case, financial) measure feigns a temporary move in the upward or downward direction.

TIP: Be weary of assuming that revenues will continue rising if they have risen year-over-year, for a couple of years. Assuming the aforementioned would constitute speculation as you are projecting optimistic prospects for the future, rather than assuming average prospects of growth. Instead, use trailing 10-year revenues and calculate the median of those data. This will always give you a lower, more conservative revenue number–

increasing your margin-of-safety and further securing any potential investment principal you are considering trading for the company's security.

Next, I would like to skip to the very bottom of the income statement to finalize this section of analysis.

At this stage of analysis, assuming the 10-year revenue data is devoid of extreme variation and has yielded a reasonable median, the enterprising analyst would move to review the company's net profit with the exact same scrutiny. Here, you are synthesizing the trailing 10-year net profit median, surveying for extreme variation, and making an artful judgement on the sufficiency of the company's net profit. An *artful judgement* entails a review for any net loss years, a sufficient explanation assuming the former, as well as a proper industry comparison checking for competitiveness.

TIP: As a shareholder, the net profit is *your* money which you can choose, via voting rights proportionally awarded from owned stock, to reinvest in the company through retained earnings or pay out to yourself, and other shareholders, in the form of dividends. It is important to remember that common stock is ownership interest in a company. As a stockholder, you partially own a company, and both the company, and its board of directors, are answerable and wholly accountable to you!

DEFINITE PROSPECTS

In 2013, Carl Frey and Michael Osborne, of the University of Oxford, published a peer-reviewed article regarding the future of jobs in America. Specifically, they calculated which jobs held the highest probability for obsolescence due to computerization (ironically, they used machine-learning AI to come to their conclusions, they should watch out!)

The famous research article can be read in its entirety here: **https://www.oxfordmartin.ox.ac.uk/downloads/academic/The_Future_of_Employment.pdf** .

Interestingly, you can search an indexed version of the paper's conclusions, job for job, at a website titled **https://willrobotstakemyjob.com/** . Search for a job of interest and see if a robot is filling out his application now.

The authors state that these probabilities are to be fulfilled over the span of "the next decade or two" and are based on intuitive concepts that delineate what a computer could or could never do. Jobs which require dexterity, or empathy, for example, are considered as having a lower probability of computerization, while jobs that are procedural in nature have a higher probability of computerization. Ultimately, they claim that "47% of U.S. employment is in the high risk category" regarding computerization; meaning that a computer program/robot could successfully do 47% of jobs in America.

In the context of a successful investment program, any reasonable person should use this peer-reviewed, evidenced-based literature as a guiding hand, narrowing the prospective securities which should be deemed as investable. In practice, it is hard to distinguish speculative behavior, with reference to identifying a firm's *definite prospects*, from rational investing behavior. However, when it comes to assessing the truth-value of claims and conclusions, this author knows of no better source of measurable truth than the truth created by the hypothetico-deductive method. As a responsible investor judging the definite prospects of a company, you should avail yourself of industry relevant information published in the online scientific libraries of universities and academic journals.

Returning to the aforementioned research article, plainly speaking, I would not invest in a company whose competitive advantage solely rests on high risk labor, as its future holds non-definite prospect. Conversely, a firm would appear investable if it could (or maybe it already has) benefit from gains in operational efficiency by restructuring inefficient labor–trading labor for robots. Granted, the company would have to be willing to lay-off/restructure their workforce. It would be very hard to find evidence in annual statements of a firms desire to computerize its workforce in the name of efficiency (that just seems cold). However, a simple Google search for "Company X layoff" or "Company X labor restructure" could assist in determining if a company has done this type of move in the past. While historical behavior does not guarantee future behavior, in this case, the past may indicate the future. The bible illuminates this concept in Ecclesiastes 1:9: "What has been is what will be, and what has been done is what will be done, and there is nothing new under the sun." If a company unabashedly has transformed a workforce to survive in the past, in may do so, as well, in the future–especially if similar management is still in place!

What do Graham and Dodd have to say about *definite prospects*? A company has definite prospects if the company engages in *good business* and is led by *good management* (page xxxv of *Securities Analysis*, 6th edition).

> Good business is defined as having "strong barriers to entry, limited capital requirements, reliable customers, low risk of

> technological obsolescence, abundant growth possibility, and significant and growing free cash flow."
>
> Good management can be described (page xxxvi) as having "acumen, foresight, integrity, and motivation".

Further comment from Graham on definite prospects leads to conversation surrounding blue-chip stocks, or stocks which are regarded highly by the public–renowned for their reliability and profitability. The public seems to be mostly convinced that blue-chip stocks are perpetually worthy of investment–just look at any trading volume reports, you'll see the blue-chips at the very top. However, Graham is skeptical of blue-chip stocks, and their future prospects. On page 33 of the 6th edition of *Security Analysis*, Graham hypothesizes:

> But is it not possible that Wall Street has carried its partiality [for blue-chips] too far—in this as in so many other cases? May not the typical large and prosperous company be subject to a twofold limitation: first, that its very size precludes spectacular further growth; second, that its high rate of earnings on invested capital makes it vulnerable to attack if not by competition then perhaps by regulation?

The aggregate of value-investing literature warns its readers of blue-chip securities trading at unjustifiable prices (ignore all the lies management tries to sell you). However, the un-skeptical individuals, whom of which regularly participate in "market folly" (refer to chapter 8 of *The Intelligent Investor*), chronically cast their votes, in the form of security purchases–blind to any fundamental indications of overpricing–and drive prices sky-high. This is what is meant by Graham, in both books, when he refers to the market as a voting machine in the short term, and a weighing machine in the long term.

This might lead you to believe that you should strictly avoid blue-chip stocks and bonds. This is wrong.

Allow me to continue battling your assumptions. You may be in a cognitive quandary where it appears that you only have the option to buy overpriced stock from a great company or buy cheap stock from a bad company. This is wrong, as well. From page 80 of *Security Analysis*, in so many words: not all big companies are safe, and not all cheap companies are bad.

Understand that when you are analyzing a stock, you are analyzing a business. Investment merit should be considered on a case-by-case basis.

To summarize this section regarding the determination of a company's *definite prospects*, a company has definite prospects if:

the company engages in good business

> strong barriers to entry, limited capital requirements, reliable customers, low risk of technological obsolescence (refer to Oxford research paper above), abundant growth possibility, and significant and growing free cash flow

> add to that, is long established (10 years or greater), well financed (high stockholders equity/low liabilities), important in it's industry (high market capitalization), destined to stay (low risk of technological obsolescence)

the company is led by good management

> acumen, foresight, integrity, and motivation

TIP: Be sure not to double count "good management" in your analysis. A clean 8-K filing (no major lawsuits), along with stable financials, can serve as a good enough indication that management is not bad.

FINAL NOTE ON INTRINSIC VALUE

While this 5th step on intrinsic value determination represents the *meat and potatoes* of value investing, it is not the last step. In a thorough fundamental analysis which identifies investment merit it is not only important to review the company's performance at face value, but to also compare the company's performance to other similar companies. Also, maintaining a skeptical eye in any investment operation serves as a competitive advantage: knowing how to check for signs of accounting fraud could save you from total loss. I will briefly review the two topics next.

6. RESEARCH **INDUSTRY COMPETITORS**

How can you be certain the company you are researching isn't coming in last place with reference to industry performance? While analyzing business fundamentals in a vacuum serves a purpose, a supplementary comparison to a firm's competitors checks for healthy business performance, as well.

It is important to know if a competing firm operates factors more efficiently, for example, because this may serve as an indication that sales of the company under scrutiny may start to decrease–as the competitor wins more market share–especially in elastic markets (where any opportunity to decrease price, and consequently increase market share, is seized by firms).

The first and most important financial benchmark to compare is the **Net Profit Margin**. Defined as net profit divided by revenue (Net Profit Margin = Net Profit/Revenue), this financial benchmark serves as the essential indication of management efficiency. This ratio describes the efficiency at which goods were sold, operational efficiency, and tax efficiency in one neat number. It is important that this ratio fall within reasonable range of the industry benchmark.

TIP: It's a myth that a better business means a larger profit margin in all cases. In fact, in a hyper-elastic market like auto insurance, if an auto-insurance company has a substantially larger profit margin over an accounting period, as compared to industry benchmarks, it means the company grossly overestimated accident risk and lost opportunity to seize market share at lower prices. This substantially larger profit margin represents mismanagement (specifically, loose underwriting) and is a cause for concern in the context of an investment considerations. Know your business! Know your industry!

The second most important financial benchmark to analyze regards liquidity. The company you are investing in should have the ability to pay it's short-term debt, with a little left over. This isn't the case for all industries, however, generally this is the favorable case. Comparing the companies **Current Ratio** to the industry benchmark avails the analyst of the surety that the company under scrutiny could weather a particularly nasty market recession. The Current Ratio is defined as current assets divided by current liabilities (Current Ratio = Current Assets/Current Liabilities).

The third financial benchmark also regards liquidity. The **Cash Ratio** (Cash and Cash Equivalents/Current Liabilities) reveals the company's sense of responsibility, to a degree, towards its creditors. This is important because, once invested, *you* will be considered among those creditors!

The fourth benchmark is a profitability ratio: the **Return on Assets Ratio**. It is important to know how efficient a firm is at generating net income from its assets–and that's exactly what this ratio measures (Return on Assets = Net Income/Assets). If a company is performing poorly, with respect to its competitors on this metric, a sufficient reason should be found. Otherwise, it may be best to park your money elsewhere.

START YOUR INDUSTRY RESEARCH

Any industry research you would like to complete can be found, for free, at this website: **https://www.readyratios.com/sec/** . Just type in the company in the search field.

7. CHECK FOR **ACCOUNTING FRAUD**

The final step is checking for any accounting red flags, potential misrepresentation, or outright fraud. This is an important part of the due diligence process–especially if you are considering a particularly large cash investment.

There is a myth that some financial statements are easier to misrepresent than others. In fact, all items on all of the required SEC filing statements can be misrepresented, flubbed, cooked, exaggerated, et cetera.

Howard Schilit, renowned forensic accountant and author of best-selling book titled *Financial Shenanigans*, shows exactly how each statement can been fraudulently misrepresented using his experience, case studies of infamous examples like Waste Management (1998), Enron (2001), Worldcom (2002) and Tyco (2002).[4] The author makes these stories read like engaging novelas. It was Jason Zweig, commenter in the revised 2006 edition of *The Intelligent Investor*, which led me to this incredible book, as toward the end of the book, he recommends it as advanced reading for his audience. Here are key take-aways from the book:

THREE TYPES OF ACCOUNTING MANIPULATION

Earnings Manipulation
Cash Flow Manipulation
Key Metric Manipulation

EARNINGS MANIPULATION

1. Recording Revenue too soon
2. Bogus Revenue
3. Boosting Revenue using one-time or unsustainable activities
4. Shifting Expenses to a later period
5. Hiding Expenses or losses
6. Shifting income to a later period
7. Shifting Expenses to current period

CASH FLOW MANIPULATION

1. Shifting Financial inflows/outflows to Operating Cash Flows
2. Moving cash flows from Operating Cash Flows to other sections
3. Boosting Operating Cash Flows using unsustainable activity

---

[4] Disclaimer: I do not own, nor claim to own, any of the intellectual property, concepts, or text in any edition and/or publication of *Financial Shenanigans*. Any reference to the aforementioned publication within this eBook serves as educational review, and is for educational purposes only.

KEY METRIC MANIPULATION

1. Showcasing non-SEC required numbers (EBITDA)
2. Distorting the Balance Sheet

Without further ado, here are some accounting fraud examples in no particular order of importance (because any accounting fraud is important):

DRAMATIC TRENDS

On page 19 of Financial Shenanigans, Schilit describes Enron's meteoric increase in revenue from 1995 to 2000. In just 5 years, Enron's annual revenue went from $10 billion to $100 billion. This is an increase by a factor of 10 in just 5 years. As Schilit describes, "this just doesn't happen." In fact, no company, in recorded history, has *ever* multiplied their revenue by a factor of 10 at the scale Enron purported in the late 90's.

Table 1-1 Enron's Revenue and Net Income, 1995 to 2000

($ millions)	**1995**	**1996**	**1997**	**1998**	**1999**	**2000**
Revenue	**9,189**	13,289	20,273	31,260	40,112	**100,789**
Net income	520	584	105	703	893	979

Credit: Financial Shenanigans, 4th Edition, Schilit, Chapter 1, Page 19

What really happened? Enron was treating trades, and their respective nominal values, like **Revenue**, and were inappropriately tweaking **Cost of Goods Sold**.

Lesson to be learned? If it's too good to be true (10X INCREASE IN SALES IN 5 YEARS), it probably is.

ACQUISITION CRAZY

Be weary of increasing revenue figures if a company's central operations are dwarfed by frequent acquisitions. This does not only indicate aging through the business lifecycle (and a weakening value proposition), but something perhaps, more sinister. Acquiring companies can use cash (acquired from the bought business) as revenue, artificially pumping the top line.

Ways to spot the fraud? Check the company's **Cash Flow from Operations**. Cash inflows from operations should be a substantial portion of the company's total inflows. This requires a global understanding of the company, and common sense.

AGGRESSIVE CHIEF

If the tone at the top embodies a cut-throat, numbers-only, culture, you should think twice about investing in the company. Schilit recounts stories of verified suspicion, initially sparked by brutish comments from c-suite executives plainly stating that nothing mattered more than making the numbers.

The author goes as far as to say that this type of metric-based, numbers-only, culture serves as a causal prerequisite for fraud. Investors beware!

SKEPTICISM IS YOUR COMPETITIVE ADVANTAGE

When reviewing financial statements, you don't need to be as thorough as a forensic accountant. Simply being healthily skeptical and asking questions like "Why?" or "Why now?" will abet your investing operation.

Always consider how the most important results would have looked *had the change not happened*. This change could be any non-normal accounting item that appears deflated or perhaps inflated. Check the notes try to read between the lines. Always remember that management is motivated to secure investor confidence–rarely will management truly disclose gory details of an operative failure in frank terms. *Integrity over metrics* is the tone you should be on the lookout for.

Also, pay attention to c-level incentive structure. Are they paying the CEO in stock-options? That's not good, because then his motivation is perversely altered, incentivizing him to drive share price up, and not drive true management performance.

Look instead for incentive structures based on improving **GAAP** items, like **Net Profit**, not share price.

QUICK REFERENCE GUIDE

1. SET THE TONE–REMEMBER THE REAL DEFINITION OF INVESTING
2. SELECT INDUSTRY BASED ON FAMILIARITY
3. PE >= 20 ABANDON, PE < 20 PROCEED
4. BOOK VALUE <= 0 ABANDON, BOOK VALUE > 0 PROCEED
5. PPS < BOOK VALUE/SHARES PROCEED, PPS >= BOOK VALUE/SHARES CAUTION
6. PPS < NCA/SHARES PROCEED, PPS >= NCA/SHARES CAUTION
7. PPS < CASH/SHARES PROCEED, PPS >= CASH/SHARES CAUTION
8. CALCULATE TRAILING 10 YEAR MEDIAN ANNUAL REVENUE
9. CALCULATE TRAILING 10 YEAR MEDIAN ANNUAL NET PROFIT
10. DOES THE COMPANY HAVE:
    1. strong barriers to entry?
    2. limited capital requirements?
    3. reliable customers?
    4. low risk of technological obsolescence?
    5. abundant growth possibility?
    6. significant and growing free cash flow?
    7. important in industry?
11. CAN YOU DESCRIBE COMPANY MANAGEMENT AS HAVING:
    1. acumen?
    2. foresight?
    3. integrity?
    4. motivation?
12. CALCULATE NET PROFIT MARGIN, COMPARE TO INDUSTRY BENCHMARK
13. CALCULATE CURRENT RATIO, COMPARE TO INDUSTRY BENCHMARK
14. CALCULATE CASH RATIO, COMPARE TO INDUSTRY BENCHMARK
15. CALCULATE RETURN ON ASSETS RATIO, COMPARE TO INDUSTRY BENCHMARK
16. REVIEW 8-K, 10-K NOTES/STATEMENTS FOR ACCOUNTING FRAUD, MISREPRESENTATION, HEAVY LITIGATION
    1. CHECK FOR DRAMATIC TRENDS
    2. CHECK ACQUISITION FREQUENCY
    3. CHECK MANAGEMENT TONE FOR AGGRESSION/CUT-THROAT NUMBERS-ORIENTATION

ABOUT THE AUTHOR

Brenden Diaz is a first-generation JD/MBA student at the State University of New York, University at Buffalo in New York. He has an incredibly supportive wife who works full-time to put him through school. He also has a Colombian mother and Dominican father who have always valued honesty in business, generosity in society, and generativity in academia. He believes **fundamental business analysis** makes a **stronger investor, business, and economy**.

If you derived value from this book please consider a donation to my **Patreon** so that I can keep writing books and making Youtube videos for you: **www.patreon.com/brendendiaz**.

Thank you for reading and *God Speed* in your investing!

DEFINITIONS

ad infinitum: again and again in the same way; forever
assets: physical or immaterial things a company owns which will provide some future economic benefit
balance sheet: a GAAP financial statement which defines a company's controlled assets, and its financing, at one point in time
corporate bond: a type of security that conditions fixed interest payments to the lender, repays principal on a fixed date; does not provide assets, claims on any profits, or voting rights
book value: the difference between a company's assets and it's liabilities; stockholders' equity
cash flow: the sum of company's cash flows from operations, financing and investing
cash flow manipulation: non-GAAP accepted alteration to the statement of cash flows
cash ratio: net cash asset account divided by current liabilities
common stock: a type of security which offers a pro rata ownership interest on assets in excess of debts; offers pro rata ownership interest on all profits in excess of legitimate deductions; offers pro rate voting rights for the election of corporate directors
competitive advantage: a condition or circumstance that puts a company in a favorable or superior business position
cost of goods sold: direct costs of producing the goods sold by the company
current ratio: a liquidity ratio that measures a company's ability to pay short-term debt; current assets divided by current liabilities; >=1 considered favorable
earnings: net profit; a company's net benefits earned over an accounting period
earnings manipulation: non-GAAP accepted alteration to the statement of cash flows
earnings-per-share: annual net profit divided by outstanding shares

expense: a cost of operations incurred by a company to generate revenue

fundamental analysis: a way of identifying the quality of an investment by defining a company's intrinsic value and comparing that to its price

Generally Accepted Accounting Principles (GAAP): accounting standard adopted by the US SEC; promotes objectivity, materiality, consistency and prudence in financial reporting

income statement: a GAAP financial statement that reports a company's financial performance over an accounting period

intrinsic value: a company's true worth, in dollars, at any one point in time

investment analyst: a person who engages in the analysis of investments and uses fundamental analysis to do so; identifier of investment merit

investment operation: an investing strategy which prioritizes safety of principal with an ample margin of safety

key metric manipulation: the obfuscation of GAAP approved financial exhibits through the promotion of non-GAAP financial exhibits

margin of safety: the discount achieved by purchasing an investment security (common stock, preferred stock, bond) at a price less than the stock's intrinsic value

net current assets: current assets minus current liabilities; ideally should be positive

net profit margin: net profit divided by revenue; a profitability measure which suggests a management's efficiency

outstanding shares: a company's stock currently owned by investors

preferred stocks: a type of security which pays a prioritized dividend and typically holds rights over assets in the event of company dissolution; considered a hybrid security

price-per-share: the cost associated with the purchase of one marketable share of a publicly-traded company

price-to-earnings ratio: share price divided by earnings per share
principal: the original sum of money risked in an investment
profit: synonymous with net profit, earnings; a company's net benefits earned over an accounting period
return on assets ratio: net income divided by total assets; profitability measure that provides how efficient assets were at generating net income
revenue: the top-line of an income statement; the income generated from a company's business operations
safety of principal: a qualitative measure of an investment's ability to fully return to the investor
security: a tradable financial asset sold by a corporation
U.S. Securities and Exchange Commission (SEC): independent federal agency responsible for enforcing federal securities laws, proposing securities rules, and regulating the securities industry in the United States.
speculation: any operation not meeting the definition of "investment operation" as defined above
stock market: the location where securities are traded, bought, sold, and exchanged
value investing: synonymous with "investment operation"; an investing strategy which prioritizes safety of principal with an ample margin of safety

THANK YOU

Muriel,

I was so incredibly lucky to have been taught accounting–for the first time in my life–in such a patient, thought-provoking, and insightful manner. You taught me the language of business and gave me the fire in my belly to never be afraid to dive deep into financial statements!

Then, when I asked for your support in my application to business and law school, you showed up for me like no one ever has. I hope to one day support a student just like how you supported for me.

Muriel T. Anderson, CPA and Clinical Associate Professor at the State University of New York, University at Buffalo, thank you from the bottom of my heart.

-Brenden

Dianna,

I will never forget the first day in your statistics class. You completely changed the way I analyze my world. You made me feel like I could tackle any challenge with tenacity, clarity of purpose, and a healthy amount of correctly-applied wit. You set the bar high and held us accountable for our own growth.

You supported me in my application to business and law school, and offered me a teaching assistantship, which I was honored to accept!

Dianna Cichocki, Clinical Assistant Professor at the State University of New York, University at Buffalo, thank you from the bottom of my heart.

-Brenden

www.ingramcontent.com/pod-product-compliance
Lightning Source LLC
Chambersburg PA
CBHW040341220526
45473CB00009B/2758